WHEN OVERTHINKING IS NOT GOOD

Recognising Harmful Overthinking and The Negative Impacts of Anxiety On the Anxious Mind and techniques to live fret-free.

Carol Chime

Table of Contents

What to Expect from this Book

Welcome to "When Overthinking is Not Good," a guide crafted to help you understand, manage, and ultimately overcome the mental loops that keep you from living your best life. In this book, you will embark on a journey through the complexities of overthinking, discovering the science behind it, recognizing harmful patterns, and learning practical strategies to transform your thought processes. Here's what you can look forward to:

A Deep Dive into Overthinking

We start by laying the foundation: what exactly is overthinking, and how does it differ from productive thinking? You'll learn to identify the subtle signs that your thoughts are becoming counterproductive and understand the psychological triggers that set off these mental spirals. By recognizing these patterns, you'll be better equipped to address them.

The Science Behind Overthinking

Ever wondered why your brain seems to get stuck on repeat? We'll delve into the fascinating science behind overthinking. You'll explore how the brain processes thoughts, the role of the default mode network (DMN), and how anxiety and stress contribute to overthinking. Armed with this knowledge, you'll see that overthinking isn't just a bad habit—it's a biological process that you can learn to manage.

Recognizing and Differentiating Thought Patterns

Through engaging examples and relatable case studies, you'll learn to differentiate between productive thinking and overthinking. Discover practical ways to shift your focus from endless analysis to constructive action. This section will empower you to break free from the cycles that keep you stuck and move forward with clarity and confidence.

Consequences Unveiled

Overthinking doesn't just stay in your head—it has real-world consequences. We'll explore the psychological, physical, social, and professional impacts of overthinking. From anxiety and insomnia to strained relationships and impaired decision-making, you'll gain a comprehensive understanding of how overthinking affects every aspect of your life. More importantly, you'll see why it's crucial to tackle this issue head-on.

Practical Strategies for Combating Overthinking

Get ready to equip yourself with an arsenal of effective tools. This book offers a wealth of strategies, including mindfulness and meditation techniques, cognitive-behavioral therapy (CBT) methods, and practical exercises designed to bring immediate relief. Learn how to quiet your mind, challenge negative thoughts, and develop healthier thinking habits. These actionable tips are designed to fit seamlessly into your daily routine, making it easier to implement lasting change.

Building Healthy Thought Patterns

Creating new, positive thinking habits is essential for long-term mental well-being. You'll discover how to establish routines that minimize overthinking, foster a positive mindset, and build resilience against stress. This section provides a roadmap to cultivate a balanced and fulfilling life, where overthinking no longer holds you back.

Inspiring Personal Stories and Testimonials

Sometimes, the best way to learn is through the experiences of others. Throughout the book, you'll find inspiring stories of individuals who have successfully managed their overthinking. From Sarah's journey to mental clarity through mindfulness to Mark's reduced anxiety with CBT and running, these real-life testimonials offer hope and practical insights. These stories demonstrate that change is possible and provide a relatable blueprint for your own journey.

A Compassionate Conclusion

As we wrap up, you'll find a heartfelt recap of key points and encouraging final thoughts. Overcoming overthinking is not about achieving perfection; it's about developing a healthier relationship with your thoughts. You'll leave with a sense of accomplishment and a clear path forward, ready to tackle the challenges ahead with confidence and resilience.

Embark on this transformative journey with "When Overthinking is Not Good." This book is your companion in understanding the intricacies of overthinking and providing you with the tools to take control of your thoughts. Whether you're looking for immediate relief or long-term strategies, this guide offers practical, science-backed solutions to help you live a more mindful, balanced, and fulfilling life. Let's begin this journey together and discover the peace of mind that awaits you.

Introduction

Overthinking is a habit that many of us fall into, often without even realising it. It's that incessant, looping dialogue in our heads, analysing and re-analyzing situations, replaying past events, or worrying about the future. Overthinking can take many forms, from dwelling on a conversation we had with a friend, wondering if we said the wrong thing, to obsessing over a mistake at work, fearing it will have catastrophic consequences. It's the mental equivalent of running on a treadmill; we exert a lot of energy but go nowhere.

When I first began to understand overthinking, it was a revelation. I saw how it affected my decisions, relationships, and overall happiness. The more I delved into the topic, the more I realised how widespread and damaging it could be. Overthinking can make small problems seem insurmountable and lead to unnecessary stress and anxiety. It often masquerades as problem-solving or being thorough, but it usually results in analysis paralysis, where we are unable to make decisions or take action.

The purpose of this book is to explore overthinking in depth: what it is, why we do it, and, most importantly, how we can stop it. Over the years, I've learned that overcoming overthinking is not about suppressing our thoughts or striving for a perpetually clear mind. Instead, it's about developing healthier thinking patterns, learning to manage our thoughts effectively, and recognizing when our thinking is working against us rather than for us.

Throughout this book, I'll share insights from psychology and neuroscience to explain the mechanisms behind overthinking. I'll also include practical strategies and exercises that have been shown to help people manage their thoughts more effectively. We'll look at mindfulness techniques, cognitive-behavioural therapy (CBT) strategies, and other tools that can help us break free from the cycle of overthinking. Additionally, I'll share personal stories and testimonials from people who have struggled with overthinking and found ways to overcome it.

One of the key points I want to emphasise is that overthinking is a learned behaviour, which means it can be unlearned. It's not something we're born with, but rather a habit we develop over time, often as a coping mechanism for stress, anxiety, or uncertainty. By understanding the root causes of our overthinking, we can start to address them directly and develop healthier ways to cope with life's challenges.

For instance, overthinking often stems from a desire for control. When we're faced with uncertainty or feel out of control, our minds try to regain a sense of control by over-analyzing every detail. This can lead to endless rumination, where we keep replaying scenarios in our minds, hoping to find a solution or prevent something bad from happening. However, this rarely brings us the clarity or peace we're seeking. Instead, it traps us in a cycle of worry and doubt.

Another common trigger for overthinking is fear of making mistakes or being judged. We might overthink our actions and decisions because we're afraid of failure or of what others will think of us. This fear can be paralysing, preventing us from taking risks or pursuing opportunities. It can also make us hyper-critical of ourselves, leading to low self-esteem and a constant sense of inadequacy.

Throughout this book, I'll explore these and other triggers of overthinking, helping you understand why you might be prone to overthinking and how you can address these underlying issues. I'll also share practical tips for managing your thoughts more effectively, such as setting boundaries on your thinking time, practising mindfulness, and challenging negative thoughts.

One of the most powerful tools for combating overthinking is mindfulness. Mindfulness involves paying attention to the present moment without judgement. It's about observing our thoughts and feelings without getting caught up in them. By practising mindfulness, we can learn to recognize when we're overthinking and gently bring our focus back to the present. This can help us break the cycle of rumination and develop a more balanced perspective on our thoughts and experiences.

Cognitive-behavioural therapy (CBT) is another effective approach for managing overthinking. CBT involves identifying and challenging negative thought patterns and replacing them with more positive and realistic ones. It's based on the idea that our thoughts, feelings, and behaviours are interconnected, and by changing our thoughts, we can change how we feel and act. In this book, I'll share CBT techniques that can help you recognize and reframe unhelpful thoughts, reducing the impact of overthinking on your life.

In addition to these techniques, I'll also include practical exercises and activities that you can try on your own. These exercises are designed to help you develop healthier thinking habits and manage your thoughts more effectively. They include journaling prompts, mindfulness practices, and CBT worksheets that you can use to work through your thoughts and feelings.

Finally, I'll share personal stories and testimonials from people who have successfully managed their overthinking. These stories provide real-life examples of how others have overcome their struggles with overthinking and found greater peace and clarity in their lives. I hope these stories inspire you and show you that it's possible to break free from the cycle of overthinking.

As you read this book, I encourage you to keep an open mind and be patient with yourself. Changing your thinking habits takes time and effort, but it's worth it. By understanding overthinking and learning how to manage it, you can improve your mental and emotional well-being, make better decisions, and live a more fulfilling life.

Remember, the goal is not to eliminate all thoughts or achieve a state of perfect mental clarity. Instead, it's about developing a healthier relationship with your thoughts, recognizing when they're helpful and when they're not, and taking steps to manage them effectively. I'm excited to take this journey with you and help you discover the tools and strategies you need to overcome overthinking and live a happier, more balanced life.

Chapter 1: Understanding Overthinking

What is Overthinking?

Overthinking is more than just thinking a lot; it's an unproductive mental habit that involves dwelling excessively on a single thought or a series of thoughts, often leading to mental exhaustion. It's the relentless mental chatter that can keep us awake at night, replaying past events, worrying about future possibilities, or obsessing over every little detail of our daily lives. When we overthink, we become stuck in a loop, analysing and reanalyzing situations to the point where it becomes counterproductive.

Consider this: you're preparing for a presentation at work. Instead of focusing on your content, you start worrying about all the things that could go wrong. What if you forget your lines? What if the technology fails? What if the audience doesn't respond well? This kind of thinking goes beyond preparation; it becomes a paralysing cycle of worry that can undermine your confidence and performance.

Overthinking can be broken down into two main types: rumination and worry. Rumination involves dwelling on past events, often with a focus on mistakes or perceived failures. This can lead to feelings of regret, guilt, or sadness. Worry, on the other hand, is focused on future events and often involves a sense of dread or anxiety about what might happen. Both forms of overthinking can significantly impact our mental health and quality of life.

Common Triggers of Overthinking

Understanding the common triggers of overthinking is crucial in learning how to manage it. Several factors can prompt overthinking, and these can vary from person to person. Here are some common triggers:

1. Uncertainty: When faced with the unknown, our minds naturally try to make sense of it. This can lead to overthinking as we try to anticipate every possible outcome and prepare for it. For instance, waiting for test results or navigating a job transition can trigger excessive worry and speculation.

2. Perfectionism: Perfectionists tend to overthink because they set extremely high standards for themselves and fear failure. This can lead to constant self-criticism and doubt. For example, a perfectionist might spend hours agonizing over a minor mistake in a report, fearing it will reflect poorly on their abilities.

3. Past Trauma: People who have experienced trauma may overthink as a way to regain a sense of control. Reliving the traumatic event repeatedly in their minds,

they hope to find a way to avoid similar situations in the future. This can be particularly common in individuals with post-traumatic stress disorder (PTSD).

4. Lack of Confidence: Low self-esteem can make us question our decisions and abilities, leading to overthinking. When we doubt ourselves, we might replay conversations or decisions in our heads, looking for signs that we made a mistake or that others are judging us.

5. High Stress Levels: Stressful situations can trigger overthinking as we try to navigate and cope with the challenges we face. During times of high stress, our brains go into overdrive, attempting to find solutions to our problems, but often getting stuck in a cycle of worry instead.

6. Social Media: The constant comparison to others on social media can lead to overthinking about our own lives and

choices. Seeing curated highlights of others' lives can make us question our own achievements and happiness, leading to feelings of inadequacy and excessive self-reflection.

Psychological and Emotional Impacts

The psychological and emotional impacts of overthinking are profound and wide-ranging. Chronic overthinking can take a serious toll on our mental health, contributing to a range of issues such as anxiety, depression, and chronic stress.

1. Anxiety: Overthinking often leads to anxiety because it involves focusing on potential problems and worst-case scenarios. When we constantly worry about what might go wrong, we can start to feel overwhelmed and anxious. This can manifest as physical symptoms like a racing heart, sweaty palms, and difficulty breathing.

2. Depression: Rumination, a form of overthinking focused on past events, is closely linked to depression. When we dwell on past mistakes or negative experiences, it can lead to feelings of hopelessness and sadness. This negative thought pattern can become a vicious cycle, making it difficult to move forward and enjoy life.

3. Stress: Overthinking can keep our minds in a constant state of alert, which can lead to chronic stress. This prolonged state of stress can have physical effects on the body, such as headaches, muscle tension, and fatigue. It can also weaken the immune system, making us more susceptible to illness.

4. Impaired Decision-Making: When we overthink, we can become paralyzed by indecision. The more we analyze and question our choices, the harder it becomes to make a decision. This can lead to missed

opportunities and increased stress as we struggle to commit to a course of action.

5. Sleep Disturbances: Overthinking can make it difficult to fall asleep or stay asleep. When our minds are racing with thoughts and worries, it can be hard to relax and unwind. This can lead to insomnia and poor sleep quality, which in turn can affect our mood, energy levels, and overall health.

6. Impact on Relationships: Overthinking can strain our relationships with others. When we constantly question our interactions and worry about what others think of us, it can lead to misunderstandings and conflict. It can also make it hard to be present and enjoy time with loved ones, as our minds are preoccupied with worries and doubts.

Understanding the triggers and impacts of overthinking is the first step toward managing it. By recognizing when we are overthinking and understanding why it happens, we can begin to develop strategies to break the cycle. In the following chapters, we'll explore practical techniques and tools to help manage overthinking, improve our mental health, and live a more balanced and fulfilling life. This journey is about learning to take control of our thoughts rather than letting them control us. It's about finding peace in the present moment and developing a healthier, more positive mindset.

Chapter 2: The Science Behind Overthinking

Overthinking is more than just a habit; it's a deeply ingrained cognitive process that can be explained by understanding the underlying mechanisms in our brain. This chapter delves into the science behind overthinking, exploring how our brain processes thoughts, the role of anxiety and stress, and the broader impact on our mental health.

How the Brain Processes Thoughts

Understanding how the brain processes thoughts is crucial to grasping why we sometimes fall into the trap of overthinking. Our brain is a complex organ, home to approximately 86 billion neurons, each capable of forming thousands of connections with other neurons. These connections create vast networks that underpin our ability to think, remember, and experience emotions.

When we think, neurons in the cerebral cortex, the brain's outer layer responsible for higher-order functions, fire in specific patterns. These electrical impulses travel across synapses, the tiny gaps between neurons, creating a cascade of neural activity that represents our thoughts. The prefrontal cortex, located at the front of the brain, plays a pivotal role in this process. It's involved in decision-making, planning, and moderating social behavior, acting as the brain's control center.

However, the brain's thought processes are not always straightforward. They can be influenced by various factors, including emotions, memories, and external stimuli. For instance, when we reflect on past experiences or worry about future events, the brain's default mode network (DMN) becomes active. The DMN is a network of interacting brain regions that is more active when we are at rest and not focused on the external environment. This network is responsible for self-referential thinking, such as daydreaming, reflecting on the past, and imagining the future.

In individuals who overthink, the DMN can become overactive, leading to excessive rumination and worry. This overactivity creates a loop where thoughts continuously recycle, making it difficult to break free. It's like having a song stuck in your head, but instead of a catchy tune, it's a series of worries and doubts that play on repeat. This understanding helps us see overthinking not just as a bad habit but as a biological process that we can learn to manage.

The Role of Anxiety and Stress

Anxiety and stress are significant contributors to overthinking. These emotional states not only trigger overthinking but also amplify its effects, creating a challenging cycle to break.

Anxiety is a natural response to perceived threats, an evolutionary mechanism designed to prepare the body to deal with danger. In the modern world, these threats are often psychological rather than physical – like fear of failure, social rejection, or uncertainty about the future. When we perceive a threat, the amygdala, a small almond-shaped structure in the brain, activates the fight-or-flight response. This response floods the body with stress hormones such as adrenaline and cortisol, preparing us to react quickly.

While this response is beneficial in genuinely dangerous situations, it becomes problematic when triggered by everyday stresses. The heightened state of alertness can lead to hyper-vigilance, where we become excessively aware of potential threats and start to overthink every possible outcome. For instance, before a big presentation, we might worry about forgetting our lines, technical failures, or negative audience reactions. This constant worry can lead to a cascade of negative thoughts, each building on the last, creating an overwhelming mental storm.

Stress, too, plays a significant role in overthinking. Chronic stress keeps the body in a constant state of alert, similar to anxiety, which can make it difficult to relax and focus. When we're stressed, our brain's ability to process information and make decisions is impaired. The prefrontal cortex, which is crucial for logical thinking and decision-making, becomes less effective under stress. This can lead to increased rumination, as we struggle to find solutions to our problems but find ourselves stuck in a loop of worry and doubt.

Understanding the role of anxiety and stress in overthinking highlights the importance of managing these emotional states. Techniques such as mindfulness, deep breathing exercises, and cognitive-behavioral strategies can help reduce anxiety and stress, thereby decreasing the tendency to overthink.

Impact on Mental Health

The psychological and emotional impacts of overthinking are profound and far-reaching. Chronic overthinking can take a serious toll on our mental health, contributing to a range of issues such as anxiety disorders, depression, and chronic stress.

Overthinking is closely linked to anxiety disorders. The constant cycle of worry and rumination can exacerbate feelings of anxiety, making it difficult to relax and enjoy life. Individuals who overthink often experience heightened levels of stress hormones, which can lead to physical symptoms such as headaches, muscle tension, and fatigue. Over time, this constant state of anxiety can lead to more severe mental health issues, such as generalized anxiety disorder (GAD) or panic disorder.

Depression is another common outcome of chronic overthinking. When we ruminate on past mistakes or negative experiences, it can lead to feelings of hopelessness and sadness. This negative thought pattern can become a vicious cycle, making it difficult to break free and move forward. Individuals who overthink often struggle with low self-esteem and self-worth, as they constantly question their decisions and abilities.

Chronic stress is also a significant consequence of overthinking. The body's prolonged response to stress can weaken the immune system, making us more susceptible to illnesses. It can also lead to burnout, where we feel physically and emotionally exhausted, and unable to cope with daily demands. This state of constant stress can impact every aspect of our lives, from our relationships and work performance to our overall well-being.

The impact of overthinking on mental health underscores the importance of developing strategies to manage and reduce this tendency. By understanding the science behind overthinking and its effects, we can begin to take steps to break the cycle and improve our mental health. In the following chapters, we will explore practical techniques and tools to help manage overthinking, improve mental resilience, and live a more balanced and fulfilling life. This journey is about learning to take control of our thoughts rather than letting them control us, finding peace in the present moment, and developing a healthier, more positive mindset.

Chapter 3: Recognizing Harmful Overthinking Patterns

Understanding overthinking is the first step, but recognizing when it becomes harmful is crucial for managing it effectively. Overthinking can be subtle and often goes unnoticed until it starts to impact our daily lives. This chapter focuses on identifying the signs of overthinking, differentiating between productive thinking and overthinking, and sharing case studies and examples to illustrate these concepts.

Identifying Signs of Overthinking

Recognizing the signs of overthinking can be challenging, especially since thinking and reflection are natural parts of the human experience. However, there are specific patterns and behaviors that indicate when thinking has crossed the line into overthinking.

One of the primary signs of overthinking is excessive rumination. This involves repeatedly replaying events in your mind, analyzing every detail, and questioning your actions and decisions. For instance, after a social interaction, you might find yourself obsessively thinking about what you said, how others reacted, and whether you made a good impression. This type of thinking often leads to feelings of regret and self-doubt.

Another sign of overthinking is constant worry about the future. This can manifest as imagining worst-case scenarios for upcoming events or decisions. You might find yourself stuck in a loop of "what if" questions, fearing negative outcomes that may never happen. This form of overthinking can cause significant anxiety and prevent you from enjoying the present moment.

Overthinking can also lead to difficulty making decisions. When faced with a choice, you might analyze every possible outcome, considering all the pros and cons, until you feel paralyzed by indecision. This can happen with both small and large decisions, from choosing what to eat for dinner to making career moves.

Physical symptoms can also be indicators of overthinking. These include headaches, muscle tension, and difficulty sleeping. If you find yourself lying awake at night, unable to quiet your mind, it's likely that overthinking is at play. Similarly, if you notice that your body is tense or you experience frequent headaches, it could be a sign that your mind is working overtime.

Differentiating Between Productive Thinking and Overthinking

Not all thinking is harmful. In fact, reflective thinking and planning are essential for problem-solving and personal growth. The key is to differentiate between productive thinking and overthinking.

Productive thinking is goal-oriented and time-limited. It involves considering a problem, generating potential solutions, and then taking action. For example, if you are planning a trip, productive thinking would involve researching destinations, booking accommodations, and creating an itinerary. Once these tasks are completed, you move on to other things.

Overthinking, on the other hand, lacks a clear goal and often goes on indefinitely. It involves excessive analysis without reaching a conclusion or taking action. Using the same example of planning a trip, overthinking would involve obsessing over every detail, such as weather forecasts for each day, the potential for flight delays, and whether you've chosen the best hotel, to the point where you feel overwhelmed and unable to enjoy the anticipation of your vacation.

A helpful way to differentiate between productive thinking and overthinking is to ask yourself whether your thoughts are leading to action or just more thoughts. Productive thinking results in decisions and actions that move you forward, whereas overthinking keeps you stuck in a cycle of analysis and doubt.

Another distinction is the emotional impact. Productive thinking tends to be empowering and positive, giving you a sense of control and direction. Overthinking, in contrast, is often accompanied by negative emotions such as anxiety, fear, and self-doubt. If your thinking is making you feel worse rather than better, it's a sign that you may be overthinking.

Case Studies

To illustrate the difference between productive thinking and overthinking, let's look at a few case studies.

Case Study 1: Sarah's Job Interview

Sarah has an upcoming job interview for a position she really wants. In preparation, she spends time researching the company, practicing her responses to common interview questions, and planning her outfit. This is productive thinking. However, the night before the interview, she starts to worry about every possible thing that could go wrong. She imagines stumbling over her words, forgetting key points, or being asked questions she can't answer. She lies awake for hours, replaying potential scenarios in her mind. This is overthinking. The next day, she's exhausted and anxious, which affects her performance in the interview.

Case Study 2: Mark's Presentation

Mark has to give a presentation at work. He prepares thoroughly, creating detailed slides and practicing his speech multiple times. This productive thinking helps him feel confident and ready. However, after the presentation, he starts to overthink every moment. He wonders if his colleagues noticed the small mistake he made on one slide, or if they thought he was nervous. He spends the entire evening replaying the presentation in his mind and worrying about what others thought of him. This overthinking causes him unnecessary stress and detracts from his accomplishment.

Case Study 3: Emily's Social Interaction

Emily meets up with friends for dinner. During the evening, she enjoys the conversation and feels relaxed. Later that night, she begins to overthink the interaction. She worries that she talked too much, or that she said something that might have offended someone. She replays the entire evening in her mind, scrutinizing every word and gesture. This overthinking makes her anxious and prevents her from enjoying the positive experience she had.

These examples highlight how overthinking can turn positive or neutral situations into sources of stress and anxiety. By recognizing these patterns, we can start to develop strategies to manage overthinking and focus on more productive and positive thinking habits.

Recognizing harmful overthinking patterns is the first step towards managing them. By identifying the signs, differentiating between productive thinking and overthinking, and learning from real-life examples, we can begin to break the cycle of overthinking and improve our mental and emotional well-being. The following chapters will provide practical tools and strategies to help you manage your thoughts

more effectively and lead a more balanced,
fulfilling life.

Chapter 4: Consequences of Overthinking

Overthinking might seem like a harmless habit, but it can have profound and far-reaching consequences on various aspects of our lives. This chapter explores the psychological effects, physical effects, social and interpersonal consequences, professional implications, impact on relationships, and overall influence on physical health.

Psychological Effects: Anxiety and Stress

One of the most immediate psychological effects of overthinking is increased anxiety. When we overthink, we often focus on worst-case scenarios, potential failures, and hypothetical problems. This relentless cycle of worry can trigger anxiety, a state characterized by persistent feelings of apprehension and fear. Over time, this can lead to chronic anxiety disorders, which are marked by excessive, uncontrollable worry that interferes with daily life.

Stress is another significant psychological effect of overthinking. The brain, under constant pressure to analyze and predict outcomes, releases stress hormones like cortisol. While cortisol can be helpful in short bursts, chronic overthinking keeps the body in a prolonged state of stress, leading to fatigue, irritability, and a host of other mental health issues. This constant state of stress can also impair cognitive functions, making it difficult to concentrate, remember details, and make decisions.

Physical Effects: Insomnia

The physical effects of overthinking can be just as debilitating as the psychological ones. One of the most common physical consequences is insomnia. Overthinking often leads to racing thoughts that make it hard to fall asleep or stay asleep. You might find yourself lying in bed, replaying events from the day, worrying about tomorrow, or even thinking about things that happened years ago.

Chronic insomnia can have severe repercussions on overall health. Lack of sleep affects everything from cognitive function to mood regulation. It can lead to increased irritability, decreased productivity, and a weakened immune system. Over time, sleep deprivation can contribute to serious health conditions such as hypertension, diabetes, and heart disease.

Social and Interpersonal Consequences: Isolation and Withdrawal

Overthinking can also strain social and interpersonal relationships. When we overthink social interactions, we may start to second-guess our words and actions, worrying excessively about how others perceive us. This can lead to social anxiety, where the fear of being judged or making a mistake becomes so overwhelming that we avoid social situations altogether.

As a result, overthinking can lead to isolation and withdrawal. We might decline invitations, avoid gatherings, or limit our interactions with others. This self-imposed isolation can exacerbate feelings of loneliness and depression, creating a vicious cycle where the more we overthink, the more isolated we become, and the more isolated we become, the more we overthink.

Professional Implications: Impaired Decision Making

In the professional realm, overthinking can severely impair decision-making abilities. When faced with a decision, overthinkers tend to analyze every possible outcome and scenario, often to the point of paralysis. This analysis paralysis can delay decision-making and hinder productivity. In a work environment, where timely decisions are crucial, this can lead to missed opportunities and decreased performance.

Moreover, overthinking can erode confidence in one's professional abilities. Constantly doubting decisions and fearing negative outcomes can make it difficult to take risks or pursue new opportunities. This lack of confidence can be visible to colleagues and superiors, potentially affecting career progression and workplace relationships.

Impact on Relationships

Relationships, whether romantic, familial, or platonic, can suffer greatly from the effects of overthinking. When we overthink interactions and conversations, we may start to misinterpret the intentions and actions of those around us. This can lead to misunderstandings, conflicts, and unnecessary tension.

For example, overthinking can cause us to read too much into a partner's offhand comment or a friend's delayed response to a message. We might start to question their feelings or loyalty, leading to mistrust and insecurity. These negative thought patterns can erode the foundation of trust and communication that is essential for healthy relationships.

In more severe cases, overthinking can lead to controlling or clingy behavior, as we try to mitigate our fears and insecurities. This can push loved ones away and create a self-fulfilling prophecy, where our fears of rejection or abandonment become a reality due to our overthinking-induced behaviours.

Influence on Physical Health

The influence of overthinking on physical health extends beyond insomnia. The constant release of stress hormones like cortisol can have several adverse effects on the body. Chronic stress can weaken the immune system, making us more susceptible to infections and illnesses. It can also increase inflammation in the body, which is linked to various chronic diseases such as arthritis, cardiovascular disease, and even some forms of cancer.

Moreover, overthinking can lead to unhealthy coping mechanisms such as overeating, smoking, or excessive alcohol consumption. These behaviors, in turn, have their own detrimental effects on physical health. For instance, stress eating can lead to weight gain and related health issues like diabetes and hypertension, while smoking and excessive drinking can cause respiratory and liver diseases, respectively.

Additionally, the physical manifestations of overthinking, such as headaches, muscle tension, and digestive issues, can significantly reduce the quality of life. Constantly feeling physically unwell can further perpetuate stress and anxiety, creating a feedback loop that is hard to break.

The consequences of overthinking are far-reaching, impacting our psychological well-being, physical health, social interactions, professional life, and relationships. Recognizing these effects is the first step toward managing and mitigating them. The following chapters will provide practical tools and strategies to help break the cycle of overthinking, fostering a healthier, more balanced approach to thinking and living. By understanding the science and consequences of overthinking, we can empower ourselves to take control of

our thoughts and improve our overall
quality of life.

Chapter 5: Strategies to Combat Overthinking

Overthinking can feel like a relentless mental hamster wheel, but there are effective strategies to help break this cycle. This chapter focuses on practical methods such as mindfulness and meditation techniques, Cognitive Behavioral Therapy (CBT) techniques, and various practical exercises and tips to manage and reduce overthinking.

Mindfulness and Meditation Techniques

Mindfulness and meditation are powerful tools for combating overthinking. They help by grounding you in the present moment, reducing the incessant chatter of the mind. At its core, mindfulness is about paying attention to the present without judgment. It involves being aware of your thoughts, feelings, and surroundings, and accepting them as they are.

One of the simplest mindfulness practices is mindful breathing. This technique involves focusing your attention on your breath, noticing the sensation of air entering and leaving your body. When your mind starts to wander, as it inevitably will, gently bring your focus back to your breathing. This practice can help calm the mind and reduce the tendency to get caught up in overthinking.

Body scan meditation is another effective mindfulness technique. This involves lying down or sitting comfortably and focusing on each part of your body, starting from your toes and moving up to your head. As you focus on each area, notice any sensations, tensions, or discomfort without trying to change anything. This practice helps increase body awareness and can be very grounding, helping to pull you out of your head and into the present moment.

Mindful walking is also a great way to incorporate mindfulness into your daily routine. As you walk, pay attention to the sensation of your feet touching the ground, the movement of your legs, and the rhythm of your breath. Notice the sights, sounds, and smells around you. This practice not only helps reduce overthinking but also allows you to appreciate the world around you.

Meditation practices, such as loving-kindness meditation, can also be beneficial. This involves sitting quietly and focusing on cultivating feelings of compassion and love, first towards yourself and then extending those feelings to others. This practice can help reduce negative self-talk and increase feelings of connectedness and positivity.

Cognitive Behavioral Therapy (CBT) Techniques

Cognitive Behavioral Therapy (CBT) is a highly effective approach for managing overthinking. CBT focuses on identifying and challenging negative thought patterns and beliefs, and replacing them with more balanced and realistic ones.

One of the core techniques of CBT is cognitive restructuring. This involves identifying automatic negative thoughts and examining the evidence for and against these thoughts. For example, if you find yourself thinking, "I always mess things up," cognitive restructuring would involve looking for evidence that disproves this thought, such as times when you succeeded or did something well. This helps to weaken the hold of negative thinking patterns and fosters a more balanced perspective.

Another useful CBT technique is thought stopping. When you catch yourself overthinking, you can use a mental or physical cue to interrupt the thought process. For example, you might say "stop" out loud or visualize a stop sign. This helps to break the cycle of rumination and shift your focus to more productive thoughts.

Behavioral activation is another key CBT technique that can help combat overthinking. This involves identifying and engaging in activities that you enjoy and that give you a sense of accomplishment. By keeping yourself engaged in positive activities, you can reduce the time and energy spent on overthinking.

Journaling is also a powerful CBT tool. Writing down your thoughts and feelings can help you gain perspective and clarity. It allows you to explore your thoughts in a structured way and can be particularly helpful in identifying patterns of overthinking. You might find it useful to write about what triggered your overthinking, how it made you feel, and what you can do differently next time.

Practical Exercises and Tips

In addition to mindfulness and CBT techniques, there are various practical exercises and tips that can help manage overthinking.

Set Time Limits for Worrying: Allocate a specific time each day to focus on your worries, such as 15 minutes in the evening. During this time, allow yourself to think about whatever is bothering you. Once the time is up, redirect your attention to other activities. This helps contain overthinking to a designated period, preventing it from taking over your entire day.

Practice Gratitude: Focusing on what you are grateful for can help shift your mind away from negative thoughts. Each day, write down three things you are grateful for. This practice can help reframe your thinking and foster a more positive outlook.

Engage in Physical Activity: Exercise is a great way to break the cycle of overthinking. Physical activity releases endorphins, which can improve your mood and reduce stress. Whether it's going for a run, taking a yoga class, or simply going for a walk, moving your body can help clear your mind.

Limit Exposure to Triggers: Identify what triggers your overthinking and try to limit your exposure to these triggers. For example, if certain social media platforms make you anxious, consider taking a break from them. If specific situations or people trigger overthinking, find ways to manage these interactions more effectively.

Focus on Problem-Solving: Instead of ruminating on problems, shift your focus to finding solutions. Break down the issue into smaller, manageable parts and brainstorm possible solutions. Taking action, even small steps, can help you feel more in control and reduce overthinking.

Seek Social Support: Talking to someone you trust about your thoughts and worries can be very helpful. Sometimes just expressing your concerns can provide relief. Friends and family can offer support and perspective that you might not have considered.

Practice Self-Compassion: Be kind to yourself. Recognize that everyone overthinks at times, and it's a normal part of being human. Instead of criticizing yourself for overthinking, practice self-compassion. Acknowledge your feelings and remind yourself that it's okay to feel this way.

Establish a Routine: Having a daily routine can provide structure and help reduce the time available for overthinking. When your day is planned out, you are less likely to spend idle time caught up in your thoughts.

Use Visualization Techniques: Visualize yourself successfully managing overthinking and coping with stress. Imagine a peaceful place or a positive outcome. Visualization can help reduce anxiety and build confidence.

Combating overthinking requires a multifaceted approach, combining mindfulness, CBT techniques, and practical exercises. By integrating these strategies into your daily life, you can develop healthier thinking patterns, reduce anxiety, and improve your overall mental well-being. Remember, the goal is not to eliminate thinking altogether but to cultivate a balanced and constructive approach to managing your thoughts. This journey towards mental clarity and peace is ongoing, but with consistent effort, it is entirely achievable.

Chapter 6: Building Healthy Thought Patterns

Overthinking can be a significant barrier to mental well-being, but with effort and the right strategies, it's possible to cultivate healthier thought patterns. This chapter explores how to develop positive thinking habits, establish routines to minimize overthinking, and implement long-term strategies for maintaining mental well-being.

Developing Positive Thinking Habits

Developing positive thinking habits is a foundational step towards overcoming overthinking. Positive thinking doesn't mean ignoring life's challenges but rather approaching them with a mindset that focuses on solutions and possibilities rather than problems and limitations.

One effective way to develop positive thinking habits is through gratitude practice. Start or end your day by listing three things you're grateful for. These can be as simple as a good cup of coffee in the morning or as significant as a supportive friend. This practice shifts your focus from what's wrong to what's right in your life, fostering a more positive outlook.

Affirmations are another powerful tool. Positive affirmations are statements that you repeat to yourself to challenge and overcome self-sabotaging and negative thoughts. For example, saying, "I am capable and strong," can help build self-confidence and reduce the tendency to overthink. Write down a few affirmations that resonate with you and repeat them daily, especially when you catch yourself falling into negative thought patterns.

Reframing is another essential technique. It involves changing the way you look at a situation to see it in a more positive light. For example, instead of thinking, "I failed at this task," you can reframe it as, "I learned what doesn't work, and now I can try a new approach." This shift in perspective can transform challenges into opportunities for growth and learning.

Surrounding yourself with positivity can also make a big difference. Spend time with people who uplift and support you. Engage in activities that bring you joy and fulfillment. This positive environment can reinforce healthier thinking patterns and reduce the impact of overthinking.

Establishing Routines to Minimise Overthinking

Routines can provide structure and predictability, which are powerful antidotes to overthinking. When your day is planned out, there is less time and mental space for excessive worrying.

Start by creating a morning routine that sets a positive tone for the day. This could include practices like meditation, journaling, or a short exercise session. These activities can help clear your mind and set a focused and calm tone for the day ahead. For example, spending just ten minutes in mindful meditation can significantly reduce stress and improve your ability to handle challenges throughout the day.

A consistent work routine is also crucial. Break your tasks into manageable chunks and set specific times for each. Use tools like to-do lists or digital planners to organize your day. Knowing what to expect and having a clear plan can reduce the tendency to overthink and procrastinate.

Incorporate regular breaks into your routine. Overthinking often happens when we are mentally fatigued. Taking short breaks to stretch, walk, or even just breathe deeply can help refresh your mind and keep overthinking at bay.

An evening routine is equally important. Wind down your day with activities that promote relaxation, such as reading, taking a warm bath, or practicing gentle yoga. Avoid screens for at least an hour before bed to help your mind relax and prepare for restful sleep. This routine can signal to your brain that it's time to shut down the overthinking and prepare for rest.

Long-term Strategies for Mental Well-being

Building healthy thought patterns is an ongoing process, and maintaining mental well-being requires long-term strategies. One of the most effective long-term strategies is continuous learning and personal growth. Engage in activities that challenge your mind and expand your horizons. This could be learning a new skill, taking up a hobby, or pursuing further education. Keeping your mind engaged in positive and constructive activities reduces the likelihood of falling into overthinking.

Regular physical activity is also crucial for mental well-being. Exercise releases endorphins, which are natural mood lifters. Aim for at least 30 minutes of moderate exercise most days of the week. This could be anything from a brisk walk to a dance class or a gym session. The key is to find activities that you enjoy, making it easier to stick with them in the long run.

Social connections play a significant role in long-term mental health. Cultivate strong relationships with family and friends. Make time for social activities and maintain regular contact with your loved ones. These connections provide support, reduce feelings of isolation, and offer different perspectives that can help counteract overthinking.

Mindfulness practices, as mentioned earlier, should also be a part of your long-term strategy. Regular mindfulness meditation can help keep your mind grounded in the present, reducing the tendency to dwell on past mistakes or future worries. Even just a few minutes of daily mindfulness can make a significant difference over time.

Therapy or counseling can be a valuable long-term investment in your mental health. A professional can help you explore underlying issues that contribute to overthinking and provide you with tools and strategies to manage it. Cognitive-behavioral therapy (CBT) and other therapeutic approaches have been proven effective in addressing overthinking and its associated anxieties.

Finally, prioritize self-care. Self-care is not a luxury but a necessity for maintaining mental health. This includes getting enough sleep, eating a balanced diet, and taking time to relax and enjoy life. Self-care practices should be tailored to your needs and preferences, ensuring that you regularly take time to nurture your body, mind, and spirit.

Building healthy thought patterns requires commitment and practice, but the rewards are profound. By developing positive thinking habits, establishing routines to minimize overthinking, and implementing long-term strategies for mental well-being, you can transform your relationship with your thoughts. This journey towards mental clarity and resilience is not about eliminating challenges but equipping yourself with the tools to navigate them effectively. Embrace these strategies, and you'll find yourself on a path to a more balanced, fulfilling, and mentally healthy life.

Chapter 7: Personal Stories and Testimonials

Reading about the science behind overthinking and learning strategies to combat it is incredibly valuable, but nothing resonates quite like hearing real-life experiences. In this chapter, we'll explore personal stories of overcoming overthinking, highlighting success stories and the lessons learned along the way. These narratives provide inspiration and practical insights, showing that change is possible and offering hope to those still struggling.

Real-life Experiences of Overcoming Overthinking

Sarah's Journey to Mental Clarity

Sarah, a 34-year-old marketing executive, struggled with overthinking for most of her adult life. She describes herself as a perfectionist, often staying up late replaying conversations and worrying about her performance at work. This constant rumination began to affect her sleep, her mood, and her relationships.

"I used to think that overthinking was just part of who I was," Sarah recalls. "But it was exhausting, and I knew I had to do something about it."

Sarah's turning point came when she attended a mindfulness workshop at her company. The facilitator introduced techniques like mindful breathing and body scans, which Sarah found surprisingly effective.

"I started practicing mindfulness every morning, just for ten minutes," she says. "It was hard at first because my mind was always racing. But over time, I learned to focus on my breath and let go of my thoughts."

Sarah also incorporated cognitive-behavioral techniques, such as cognitive restructuring, into her daily routine. She began challenging her automatic negative thoughts and replacing them with more balanced perspectives.

"Whenever I caught myself thinking, 'I'm going to mess this up,' I would stop and ask myself, 'What's the evidence for this? What's the evidence against it?' It really helped me see things more clearly."

Today, Sarah feels more in control of her thoughts and less consumed by worry. "I'm not perfect, and I still have moments of overthinking, but I don't let it control me anymore. I've learned to manage it, and it's made a huge difference in my life."

Mark's Path to Reduced Anxiety

Mark, a 28-year-old software developer, found that his overthinking was rooted in anxiety. He would constantly worry about future events, often imagining the worst-case scenarios. This habit led to frequent panic attacks and a pervasive sense of dread.

"I knew I had to change when I started avoiding things I used to enjoy because of my anxiety," Mark shares. "I was missing out on life."

Mark sought help from a therapist who specialized in CBT. Through therapy, he learned about thought stopping and behavioral activation. He began to recognize his negative thought patterns and use techniques to interrupt them.

"My therapist taught me to visualize a stop sign whenever I started to spiral. It sounds simple, but it really helped. It gave me a way to break the cycle."

In addition to therapy, Mark embraced physical activity as a coping mechanism. He took up running and found it incredibly therapeutic.

"Running became my escape and my meditation. It cleared my mind and helped me manage my stress."

With consistent effort, Mark's anxiety diminished, and he started to regain control over his life. "I still have anxious thoughts, but I don't let them dictate my actions. I've learned to focus on the present and take things one step at a time."

Emily's Social Confidence

Emily, a 25-year-old teacher, struggled with social anxiety that led to chronic overthinking. After every social interaction, she would replay conversations, analyzing every detail and worrying about how she was perceived.

"It was exhausting and made it hard to enjoy social situations," Emily explains. "I wanted to be more confident, but my mind wouldn't stop second-guessing everything."

Emily decided to tackle her overthinking by joining a support group for social anxiety. The group provided a safe space for her to share her experiences and learn from others.

"Hearing other people's stories helped me realize I wasn't alone. We all had similar fears, and it was comforting to know that others understood."

In the group, Emily was introduced to exposure therapy, where she gradually faced her social fears in a controlled way. She started with small steps, like making small talk with strangers, and gradually worked up to larger challenges, such as giving presentations.

"Exposure therapy was tough, but it was incredibly rewarding. Each success built my confidence and reduced my overthinking."

Emily also practiced self-compassion, learning to be kinder to herself and less critical of her social interactions. "I started to treat myself like I would a friend, with understanding and patience. It made a huge difference."

Today, Emily feels more confident in social situations and has significantly reduced her overthinking. "I still get nervous sometimes, but I don't let my thoughts control me. I've learned to enjoy the moment and let go of the need for perfection."

Success Stories and Lessons Learned

Sarah's Key Takeaways

Sarah's journey highlights the importance of mindfulness and challenging negative thoughts. Her success shows that even a small daily practice, like mindful breathing, can have a profound impact on mental clarity and emotional well-being. Sarah's lesson is that consistency and perseverance are crucial in overcoming overthinking.

Mark's Insights

Mark's experience underscores the value of seeking professional help and incorporating physical activity into daily life. His success with CBT and running demonstrates that combining therapeutic techniques with lifestyle changes can effectively manage anxiety and reduce overthinking. Mark's lesson is that taking proactive steps and finding healthy outlets for stress can lead to significant improvements in mental health.

Emily's Growth

Emily's story illustrates the power of community support and exposure therapy. By facing her fears gradually and practicing self-compassion, she was able to build social confidence and diminish her overthinking. Emily's lesson is that overcoming overthinking often requires stepping out of your comfort zone and being gentle with yourself during the process.

These personal stories and testimonials provide powerful evidence that overcoming overthinking is possible. By learning from the experiences of others, we can find inspiration and practical strategies to apply in our own lives. Remember, everyone's journey is unique, and what works for one person may not work for another. However, the common thread in these stories is the willingness to take action, seek support, and practice self-compassion. With these principles in mind, we can all make strides towards healthier thinking patterns and a more fulfilling life.

CONCLUSION

As we come to the end of this journey through the labyrinth of overthinking, it's essential to reflect on the key points we've discussed and take a moment to appreciate how far we've come. Overthinking, that relentless mental chatter, can feel like an insurmountable obstacle. However, with understanding, practical strategies, and a commitment to change, we can transform our relationship with our thoughts and reclaim our peace of mind.

We began by defining overthinking and recognizing its pervasive nature. Overthinking is not merely excessive thinking; it is the kind of thinking that traps us in cycles of worry and doubt, preventing us from living fully in the present. We explored how overthinking can manifest in different forms, such as rumination over past events or anxiety about future uncertainties. By identifying these patterns, we laid the groundwork for addressing them head-on.

Understanding the science behind overthinking was our next step. The brain's default mode network (DMN) plays a significant role in self-referential thinking, which can lead to overthinking when overactive. We learned that anxiety and stress are significant triggers, often exacerbating the tendency to overthink. The brain's response to perceived threats, releasing stress hormones like cortisol, can keep us in a state of heightened alertness, further fueling overthinking. Recognizing these physiological responses helps us see overthinking not just as a bad habit but as a biological process that can be managed.

Recognizing harmful overthinking patterns was crucial. By identifying signs such as excessive rumination, constant worry, and difficulty making decisions, we became more aware of when our thoughts were becoming counterproductive. Differentiating between productive thinking and overthinking was another important step. Productive thinking is goal-oriented and leads to action, while overthinking keeps us stuck in a loop of analysis and doubt. By making this distinction, we can begin to redirect our mental energy more effectively.

The consequences of overthinking are far-reaching. Psychologically, overthinking can lead to anxiety, depression, and chronic stress. Physically, it can manifest as insomnia, headaches, and other stress-related ailments. Socially, overthinking can strain relationships and lead to isolation. Professionally, it can impair decision-making and hinder career progress. Understanding these impacts underscores the importance of addressing overthinking to improve our overall well-being.

To combat overthinking, we explored various strategies. Mindfulness and meditation techniques help ground us in the present moment, reducing the mental chatter that fuels overthinking. Cognitive Behavioral Therapy (CBT) techniques, such as cognitive restructuring and thought stopping, provide practical tools for challenging and changing negative thought patterns. Incorporating these practices into our daily routines can make a significant difference in managing overthinking.

Building healthy thought patterns is an ongoing process. Developing positive thinking habits, such as gratitude practice and affirmations, can shift our focus from negativity to positivity. Establishing routines provides structure and predictability, reducing the mental space for overthinking. Long-term strategies for mental well-being, such as continuous learning, regular physical activity, and strong social connections, help maintain a balanced and resilient mindset.

Throughout this journey, we shared personal stories and testimonials to illustrate these concepts. Real-life experiences of overcoming overthinking provide powerful inspiration and practical insights. Whether it's Sarah's journey to mental clarity through mindfulness, Mark's path to reduced anxiety with the help of CBT and running, or Emily's social confidence gained through exposure therapy and self-compassion, these stories show that change is possible.

As we conclude, it's important to remember that overcoming overthinking is not about achieving a state of perfect mental clarity or eliminating all negative thoughts. It's about developing a healthier relationship with our thoughts, recognizing when they are helpful and when they are not, and taking steps to manage them effectively. It's a journey of self-discovery and growth, where each step forward is a victory.

Change takes time, patience, and persistence. There will be setbacks and moments of doubt, but each effort you make to manage overthinking is a step towards a healthier, more balanced life. Celebrate your progress, no matter how small, and be kind to yourself along the way. You have the tools and knowledge to make a positive change, and every small effort adds up to significant progress over time.

Imagine a life where overthinking no longer controls you. Picture waking up each day with a clear mind, feeling confident in your decisions, and enjoying the present moment without being weighed down by worries about the past or future. This is the life you are working towards, and it is entirely within your reach.

Take a deep breath and embrace the journey ahead. You are capable of transforming your thought patterns and reclaiming your peace of mind. Each day is an opportunity to practice the strategies you've learned, to be mindful, to challenge negative thoughts, and to build healthier habits. Trust in the process, and trust in yourself.

Remember, you are not alone in this journey. Seek support from friends, family, or professionals if needed. Surround yourself with positive influences and keep moving forward, one step at a time. Your efforts will pay off, and you will find yourself in a place of greater mental clarity and well-being.

In closing, I want to thank you for taking this journey through the complexities of overthinking. It takes courage to confront your thoughts and make a change, and you have shown that courage. Keep going, stay committed, and know that a healthier, more fulfilling life is possible. You have the power to change your thought patterns and improve your mental health. Embrace the journey, and let each step forward be a testament to your strength and resilience.